ULTIMATE CAR BATTLES

PORSCHE
vs. LOTUS

Colin Crum

WINDMILL
BOOKS
New York

Published in 2014 by Windmill Books, An Imprint of Rosen Publishing
29 East 21st Street, New York, NY 10010

First Edition

Produced for Windmill by Cyan Candy, LLC
Designer: Erica Clendening, Cyan Candy
Editor for Windmill: Joshua Shadowens

Photo Credits: Cover (top), p. 24 Darren Brode/Shutterstock.com; cover (bottom), pp. 8, 27 yencha/Shutterstock.com; p. 4 Maksim Toome/Shutterstock.com; pp. 5, 26 crydo/Shutterstock.com; p. 6 Boykov/Shutterstock.com; p. 7 Ritu Manoj Jethani/Shutterstock.com; p. 9 Olga Besnard/Shutterstock.com; p. 10 Radoslaw Lecyk/Shutterstock.com; pp. 11, 23 Wikimedia Commons; p. 12 Brian Snelson, via Wikimedia Commons; p. 13 Elena Dijour/Shutterstock.com; p. 14 DeepGreen/Shutterstock.com; p. 15 Stanislaw Tokarski/Shutterstock.com; p. 16 Matt Ragen/Shutterstock.com; p. 17 i4lcocl2/Shutterstock.com; p. 18 Paulo M. F. Pires/Shutterstock.com; p. 19 John Chapman, via Wikimedia Commons; p. 20 ZRyzner/Shutterstock.com; p. 21 Rosli Othman/Shutterstock.com; p. 22 S.Borisov/Shutterstock.com; p. 25 Fedor Selivanov/Shutterstock.com; p. 30 (top) Christoff/Shutterstock.com; p. 30 (bottom) Julie Lucht/Shutterstock.com.

Library of Congress Cataloging-in-Publication Data

Crum, Colin.
Porsche vs. Lotus / by Colin Crum. — First edition.
    pages cm. — (Ultimate car battles)
Includes index.
ISBN 978-1-4777-9003-8 (library) — ISBN 978-1-4777-9004-5 (pbk.) —
ISBN 978-1-4777-9005-2 (6-pack)
1. Porsche automobiles—Juvenile literature. 2. Lotus automobiles—Juvenile literature. I. Title.
TL215.P75C74 2014
629.222'2—dc23

2013023516

Manufactured in the United States of America

CSIA Compliance Information: Batch #BW14WM: For Further Information contact Windmill Books, New York, New York at 1-866-478-0556

TABLE OF CONTENTS

SPORTS CAR BATTLE!

Have you heard of Porsche? Porsche is a super famous maker of **luxury** sports cars. Any list of the best luxury sports cars will have many Porsche models near or at the top! Even top models from Mercedes-Benz, Audi, and BMW have a hard time competing with Porsches on the road or track.

However, there is a small British company known for building sports cars that **rival** Porsches! This company is Lotus. Like Porsche, Lotus

Porsche 911
Carrera GTS

Lotus Elise

has a long racing history that helps them build high-performance luxury sports cars. Lotus models are known for battling with Porsches in both performance tests and car races.

Car fans love to compare Porsche and Lotus. Both companies make cars that are fast and very easy to handle on the road. It can be hard to choose your favorite between these two!

ALL ABOUT PORSCHE

Porsche is a very famous name in the car world. For many car fans, Porsche means high-performance sports cars that are fun and easy to drive! Porsches are also known for being very stylish. Many celebrities around the world own and drive Porsches.

Porsche is also the most successful car brand in motorsports! More Porsches have won car races than cars

Porsche 911 Carrera S

Although Porsche is a super famous name, many people do not know how to pronounce it! In the United States, many people say "POHRSH." However, the correct pronunciation is "POHR-shuh."

made by any other company. Porsche also makes and sells the most racecars of any carmaker in the world.

Today's Porsche models include the 911, Boxster, Cayman, and Panamera. Porsche is based in Stuttgart, Germany. Currently, Porsche is owned by the Volkswagen Group.

Porsche 911

The 911 is Porsche's most famous model. This car is a two-door grand tourer with a rear-engine design. The 911s are available in coupe and cabriolet body styles. The 911 GT3 is a supercar designed for the road and track! Porsche has sold more than 820,000 911s since the car was first made in 1963.

THE SCOOP ON LOTUS

Lotus is a small car company with a lot of fans! Their headquarters is in Hethel, England. Lotus has been building cars for more than 60 years. Their lightweight sports cars are known for excellent **handling** on both the road and track. Lotuses are designed to perform especially well around tight corners and fast curves.

Lotus cars are also famous for being hand-built. Lotus's current road models are the Elise, Evora, Esprit, and Exige.

The Lotus Evora, shown here, has a 2+2 body style. This means it is built like a coupe with just two doors, but has seating for four passengers.

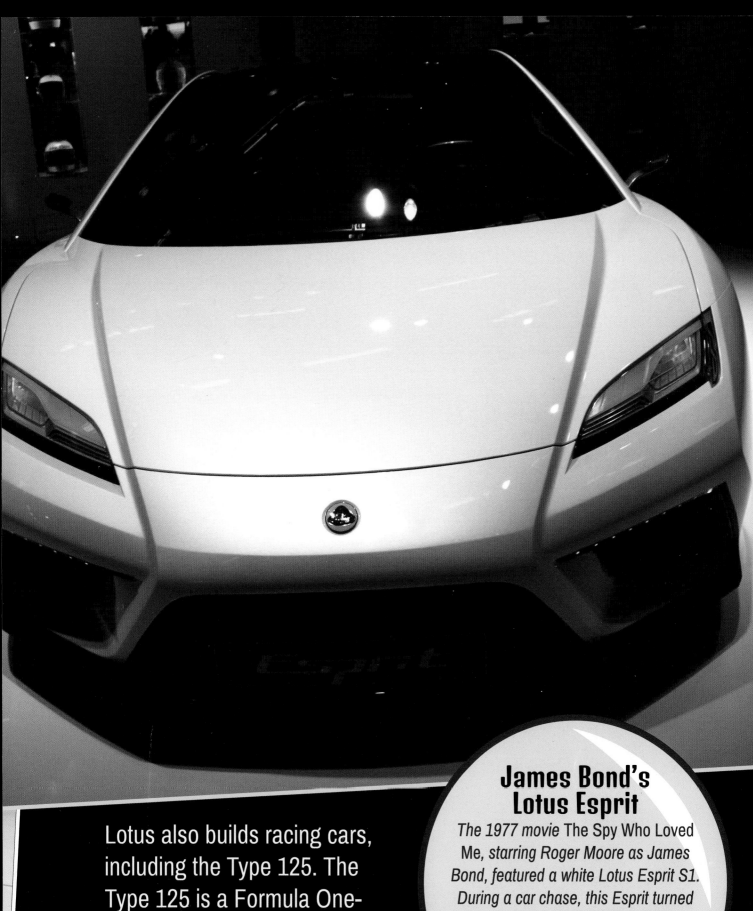

Lotus also builds racing cars, including the Type 125. The Type 125 is a Formula One-style car built to be sold to private customers! Currently, Lotus is owned by Proton.

James Bond's Lotus Esprit

The 1977 movie The Spy Who Loved Me, starring Roger Moore as James Bond, featured a white Lotus Esprit S1. During a car chase, this Esprit turned into a submarine! The film made so many people want to drive a Lotus Esprit that the car had a three-year waiting list.

PORSCHE'S BEGINNINGS

In 1948, Porsche was founded by Ferdinand Porsche. Ferdinand Porsche was a German **engineer** who designed cars for Daimler-Benz, Mercedes, and Volkswagen before making his own cars.

Porsche's first sports car was the 1948 Porsche 356.

1957 Porsche 365 Coupe

James Dean was a famous movie actor in the 1950s. He was also a fan of Porsches! Sadly, he died after crashing his Porsche 550 Spyder, such as the one shown here.

This car had an **aerodynamic** design that made it easy to handle on the road. However, its rear-mounted Volkswagen engine could produce just 40 **horsepower** (HP)!

By the 1950s, Porsche was making its own engines. The 1953 550 Spyder was a sleek, low-to-the-ground car built for racing. In 1954, Porsche built a less expensive version of the 356 called the Speedster.

In 1963, Porsche introduced a new model called the 911. Its 2-liter, 6-cylinder engine could produce 130 horsepower! When it went on sale in 1964, the 911 was an instant hit.

THE START OF LOTUS

Lotus Engineering was founded by Colin Chapman in 1952. Before starting his company, Chapman built cars for racing trials beginning in 1948. The 1952 Lotus Mark IV was the first official Lotus car. In 1953, the Lotus Mark VI racer was put into **production**.

In 1957, Lotus became famous for the Lotus Seven racecar. The Seven had a simple design that let it speed around racetracks. Lotus also

Here you can see the frame of Lotus's first production racecar, the 1953 Mark VI. Before the Mark VI, Colin Chapman only built single versions of their racecar models.

Lotus Mark Seven

introduced its first road car in 1957 at the London Motor Car Show. This 2-door coupe was the first Lotus model named the Elite. It was known for its super lightweight **fiberglass** body and frame.

In 1962, Lotus introduced a two-seat roadster with a steel frame and a fiberglass body. This car, called the Elan, had a top speed of 112 miles per hour (180 km/h).

PORSCHE OVER TIME

Over the years, Porsche designed many new models. The 912 replaced the 356 in 1965, followed by the 914 in 1970, and the 924 in 1976. In 1978, Porsche introduced the 928, powered by a 240-HP V8 engine. After its introduction in 1981, the 924 Turbo became the most popular Porsche model. In 1985, Porsche designed the high-tech 959 supercar.

This is a 1964 Porsche 356 SC, built with a powerful pushrod engine. This was the last version of the 356 Porsche built before replacing the model with the 912.

This is a Porsche 911T coupe. This version of the Porsche 911 was made between 1969 and 1973. At the time, the 911T was Porsche's most affordable 911 model.

Porsche also continued to update the 911 throughout the 1960s and 1970s. In 1982, Porsche offered the 911 SC cabriolet, the first 911 with a open roof option. The 1984 911 Carrera was sold with a high-performance 3.2-liter engine.

Porsche 959

The Porsche 959 started as a 1983 **concept car** that was put into production for 1986. This supercar was built for just like a racecar for the road! With its six-speed manual transmission and twin **turbocharger** engine, the 959 could go from 0 to 60 miles per hour (0–97 km/h) in just 3 seconds!

CHANGES FOR LOTUS

Over the years, most of Lotus's focus was on racing. However, Lotus continued to design road cars as well. In 1965, Lotus introduced a two-door grand tourer called the Europa. Like all Lotus street cars after the Elan, the Europa had a steel frame and a fiberglass body. In 1974, Lotus designed a larger version of the Elite. This Elite was a station wagon with four seats.

In 1976, the Lotus Esprit coupe became known for its aerodynamic shape and

Here is an example of a Lotus racing car! Throughout the years, racing remained Lotus's focus. Colin Chapman's love of racing is what made him want to design cars in the first place.

Vintage
Lotus Elise

amazing steering. The Esprit
went through changes in
1978 and 1980, but was
completely redesigned in
1987 with a rounder body.
A faster Turbo Esprit also
became available in 1980.

Lotus M100 Elan

In the late 1980s, Lotus wanted to design a small roadster that American drivers would want to buy. This led to the introduction of the M100 Elan in 1989. The M100 Elan was named after the 1960s Lotus Elan because the two cars shared a lightweight roadster design. The M100 Elan was known for its performance around corners.

PORSCHE IN RACING

Porsche is one of the world's most famous names in racing! Throughout the years, Porsche has won 14 maker and team world championship titles. Porsche's long racing history goes back to the 356 SL's class victory at the 1951 24 Hours of Le Mans race. In 1956, Porsche took its first overall victory with a 550 Spyder at the Targa Florio.

Here you can see a racing version of the Porsche 911 2.7. This model was named for its 2.7-liter engine. The 911 2.7 was built between 1974 and 1977.

Porsche's only Formula One victory was in 1962, when the Porsche 804 won the French Grand Prix. However, in the 1980s, Porsche built engines for McLaren Formula One cars. McLaren cars with Porsche engines took 25 Formula One wins!

Porsche's racing focus has been with long-distance and grand-touring (GT) racing. Between 1967 and 1984, Porsche took 11 wins at the Nürburgring 1000-kilometer race with 908, 910, 935, and 956 model racecars. In 1970 and 1971, Porsche had overall wins with the 917 at the 24 Hours of Le Mans.

After winning the 1998 24 Hours of Le Mans with the 911 GT1, Porsche has mostly retired from motorsports. However, they still build racecars for private teams. Porsche also took 13 wins in Le Mans Prototype Class 2 races with the Porsche RS Spyder between 2005 and 2010.

LOTUS IN RACING

Building racecars was Lotus founder Colin Chapman's favorite thing! In fact, Chapman himself raced the 1951 Lotus Mark III the year before he officially founded his company. Some of Team Lotus's early successful sports racers were the Lotus Eleven and Lotus 14 Elite, with wins at Le Mans, Sebring, and Nürburgring.

Lotus is most famous for its Formula One racers. In 1960, a Lotus 18 Formula One racer won the Monaco Grand Prix.

Here, driver Romain Grosjean of the Lotus F1 team practices for the 2013 Formula One season. This test drive took place in February 2013 at the Catalunya Circuit in Barcelona, Spain.

Team Lotus
F1 Car

Team Lotus followed up with their first victory in a Lotus 21 at the 1961 United States Grand Prix. Team Lotus driver Jim Clark won a F1 World Championship with his Lotus 25. Other innovative Lotus F1 racers included the 49, 77, and 88. Lotus was the first team to win 50 F1 Grand Prix races.

Today, a private British team competes as the Lotus F1 team. In 2013, Lotus F1 drove a Lotus E21 with a Renault engine.

GOING HEAD-TO-HEAD

Porsche and Lotus have had different racing focuses. Porsche has become famous for long-distance and GT racing, while Lotus is most famous for its Formula One racing wins. Both Porsche and Lotus are known as true racing champions!

Today, most head-to-head competitions between Porsches and Lotuses

The Lotus Evora GTE, shown here, is designed for GT2 and endurance racing. This powerful racer is built with a Toyota 3.5-liter V6 engine that can make up to 444 HP!

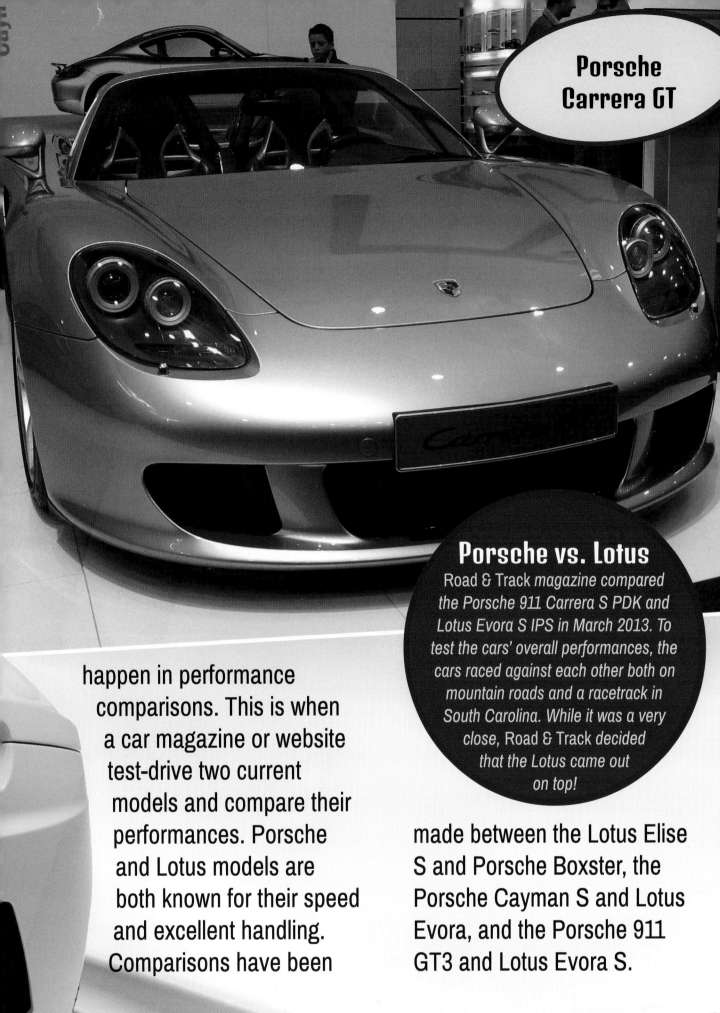

Porsche Carrera GT

Porsche vs. Lotus

Road & Track *magazine compared the Porsche 911 Carrera S PDK and Lotus Evora S IPS in March 2013. To test the cars' overall performances, the cars raced against each other both on mountain roads and a racetrack in South Carolina. While it was a very close, Road & Track decided that the Lotus came out on top!*

happen in performance comparisons. This is when a car magazine or website test-drive two current models and compare their performances. Porsche and Lotus models are both known for their speed and excellent handling. Comparisons have been made between the Lotus Elise S and Porsche Boxster, the Porsche Cayman S and Lotus Evora, and the Porsche 911 GT3 and Lotus Evora S.

Through the 1990s and 2000s, Porsche focused on driving performance and new technologies. The 1,000,000th Porsche was built in July 1996!

Today, Porsche offers three sports cars and one **sport utility vehicle** (SUV) in addition to the 911. The Boxster is Porsche's two-seat roadster, while the Cayman is a two-door coupe. The Panamera, introduced in 2010, is Porsche's first 4-door sedan. The Cayenne is a five-seat midsize crossover SUV.

This is a Porsche Cayman R, a high-performance version of the Cayman. A Cayman R built with a 7-speed manual PDK transmission can go from 0 to 60 mph (0–97 km/h) in just 4.4 seconds!

Porsche
918 RSR

High-performance **variations** are available for all of Porsche's sports car models.

Porsche also built a special edition 911 for the model's 50th **anniversary** in 2013. The 911 50 Years Edition combines modern and classic styling. Just 1,963 of these cars were built!

Porsche 918 Spyder

*For the future, Porsche is focusing on **hybrid** technology. Porsche first introduced the 918 Spyder hybrid supercar concept at the Geneva Motor Show in 2010. After improving the design, Porsche put it into production for the 2014 model year. The 918 Spyder's electric battery and V8 engine can produce more than 800 HP!*

LOTUS NOW

Lotus has designed many new exciting road models for production. However, recent money troubles have kept the line-up of Lotus road models small.

As of 2013, Lotus offered three lightweight sports car models known for their speed and handling. The Elise is a roadster with rear-wheel drive. Today, Lotus offers three versions of the Elise, including the supercharged Elise S. The Lotus Exige is a two-seat sports car built very similar to the

Lotus Exige

Here is a 2013 Lotus Elise. Its neon green color really makes it stand out! This 2-door roadster was on display at the Bangkok International Motor Show in February 2012.

Elise. The Evora is a 2+2 coupe available with either a 6-speed manual transmission or 6-speed automatic transmission.

In 2014, Lotus offered a totally redesigned Esprit supercar. The 2014 is also available with optional hybrid technology.

Lotus Ethos Concept

Lotus introduced a hybrid concept car at the Paris Motor Show in 2010. In 2011, Lotus named the concept the Lotus Ethos. The Ethos is a mini-hatchback designed with a lithium battery pack and a fuel-flex engine. Fuel-flex engines are built to run on a combination of gasoline and other fuels such as ethanol or methanol.

COMPARING CARS

Although Porsche and Lotus are both known for their high-performance sports cars, the companies have many differences.

PORSCHE

Date Founded	**1948**
First Road Model	**1948 Porsche 356**
Current Owner	**Volkswagen Group**
Headquarters	**Stuttgart, Germany**
Current Base Models in 2013–2014	**Boxster** **Cayman** **Panamera** **Cayenne** **Macan** **911** **918 Spyder**
Best 0–60 mph (0–97 km/h)	2011 Porsche 911 Turbo S 2.7 seconds
Top Speed	**2012 Porsche 911 GT2 RS** **Wimmer RS** **242 miles per hour (389 km/h)**
Most Powerful Engine	**2014 Porsche 918 Spyder** **4.6-liter V8** **608 HP**
Cars Sold in 2012	**143,096**

Just as car magazines and websites do, you too can compare and contrast Porsche and Lotus! This chart will help you look Porsche and Lotus cars over time, from the company's beginnings to today.

LOTUS

Date Founded	1952
First Road Model	1957 Lotus Elite
Current Owner	Proton
Headquarters	Hethel, England
Current Base Models in 2013–2014	Elise Exige Evora Esprit
Best 0–60 mph (0–97 km/h)	2014 Lotus Esprit 3.2 seconds (estimated)
Top Speed	1997 Lotus Elise GT1 235 miles per hour (378 km/h)
Most Powerful Engine	2014 Lotus Esprit 5-liter V8 "R-Spec" 620 HP (estimated)
Cars Sold in 2012	1,043

YOU DECIDE!

It can be hard to decide between Porsche and Lotus. Porsche is one of the most famous makers of luxury sports cars in the world! They have more racing wins than any other car brand ever. Lotus is a small company that has made a big splash with their lightweight high-performance sports cars. Lotus is also one of the most famous names in Formula One history.

Do you prefer Porsche's superfast luxury sports cars, or Lotus's lightweight cars known for their handling? Only you can decide between these two brands!

Lotus Exige

Porsche GT3 RS

GLOSSARY

aerodynamic (er-oh-dy-NA-mik) Made to move through the air easily.

anniversary (a-nuh-VURS-ree) The date on which an event occurred in the past or its special observance.

concept car (KON-sept KAR) A car to show new features and technology.

engineer (en-juh-NEER) A master at planning and building engines, machines, roads, and bridges.

fiberglass (FY-ber-glas) A material made of glass and other things.

handling (HAND-ling) Stability while driving an automobile, such as cornering and swerving.

horsepower (HORS-pow-er) The way an engine's power is measured. One horsepower is the power to lift 550 pounds (250 kg) 1 foot (.3 m) in 1 second.

hybrid (HY-brud) Cars that have an engine that runs on gasoline and a motor that runs on electricity.

luxury (LUK-shuh-ree) Comforts and beauties of life that are not necessary.

production (pruh-DUK-shun) The method of making things.

rival (RY-vul) Someone who tries to beat someone else at something.

sport utility vehicle (SPORT yoo-TIH-luh-tee VEE-huh-kul) A large car that can be driven off-road and has some other characteristics of trucks.

turbocharger (ter-boh-CHAHR-jer) A device that allows more power to the engine of a car.

variations (ver-ee-AY-shunz) A different way of doing something.

FURTHER READING

Niver, Heather. *Porsches*. Wild Wheels. New York: Gareth Stevens, 2012.

Quinlan, Julia J. *Lotus*. Speed Machines. New York: PowerKids Press, 2013.

Von Finn, Denny. *Formula 1 Cars*. Cool Rides. Minneapolis, MN: Bellwether Media, 2009.

INDEX

WEBSITES

For web resources related to the subject of this book, go to:
www.windmillbooks.com/weblinks
and select this book's title.